Mrs. Helen Motter
806 Castle Heights Rd
Bowling Green, KY 42103-8716

MORE TRIOS for Violins

22 Distinctive Arrangements of Famous Music

JOHN CACAVAS

Ode to Joy 2

Beautiful Dreamer 3

Cockles and Mussels 4

Soldier's Chorus (from the opera *Faust*) 5

Air 6

Dance of the Sugar Plum Fairy 7

The Minstrel Boy 8

Swan Lake 9

America, the Beautiful 10

Jazzy Strings 11

Tarantella 12

Streets of Laredo 13

Annie Laurie 14

O Little Town of Bethlehem 15

Eine Kleine Nachtmusik 16

(I'm A) Yankee Doodle Dandy 18

Angels We Have Heard on High 19

Havah Nagilah 20

March Militaire 21

Largo 22

Long, Long Ago 23

Amazing Grace 24

Ode to Joy

Ludwig van Beethoven
Arr. by John Cacavas

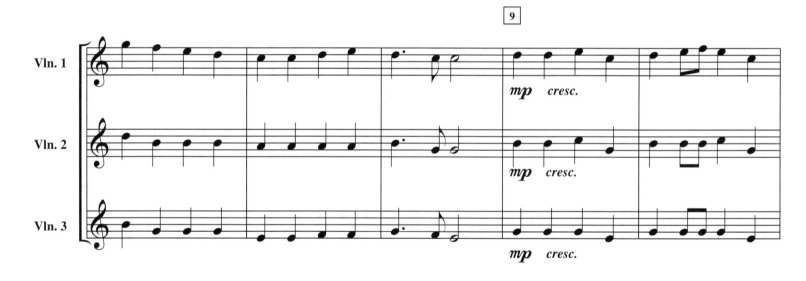

Beautiful Dreamer

Stephen Foster
Arr. by John Cacavas

Cockles and Mussels

Traditional Irish Folk Song
Arr. by John Cacavas

Soldier's Chorus

(from the opera *Faust*)

Charles Gounod
Arr. by John Cacavas

Air

Wolfgang Amadeus Mozart
Arr. by John Cacavas

Dance of the Sugar Plum Fairy

Peter Ilyich Tchaikovsky
Arr. by John Cacavas

The Minstrel Boy

Irish Air
Arr. by John Cacavas

Swan Lake

Peter Ilyich Tchaikovsky
Arr. by John Cacavas

America, the Beautiful

Samuel Ward
Arr. by John Cacavas

Jazzy Strings

by John Cacavas

Tarantella

Italian Folk Dance
Arr. by John Cacavas

Streets of Laredo

Western Folk Song
Arr. by John Cacavas

Annie Laurie

Lady John Scot
Arr. by John Cacavas

O Little Town of Bethlehem

Lewis H. Redner
Arr. by John Cacavas

Eine Kleine Nachtmusik

Wolfgang Amadeus Mozart
Arr. by John Cacavas

(I'm A) Yankee Doodle Dandy

George M. Cohan
Arr. by John Cacavas

Angels We Have Heard on High

Traditional Christmas Carol
Arr. by John Cacavas

Havah Nagilah

Jewish Folk Dance
Arr. by John Cacavas

March Militaire

Franz Schubert
Arr. by John Cacavas

Largo

Arcangelo Corelli
Arr. by John Cacavas

Long, Long Ago

Thomas Bayly
Arr. by John Cacavas

Amazing Grace

Traditional
Arr. by John Cacavas